Disclaimer

All the material contained in this book is provided for educational and informational purposes only. No reponsibility can be taken for any results or outcomes resulting from the use of this material. While every attempt has been made to provide information that is both accurate and effective,the author does not assume any responsibility for the accurasy or use/misuse of this information.

© Tasos Tsimpoukidis 2017

YouTube Channel: Tasos Tsimpoukidis

Introduction

This book is the first from an A-Z series with the goal to introduce to the kids a variety of musical instruments from all over the world.

Lets learn some instruments and a little bit about their history!

A is for Accordion

First created in Europe
in the early 1800s

B is for Balalaika

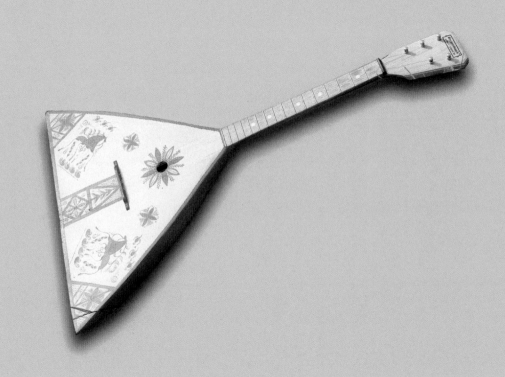

Russian stringed musical instrument with a characteristic triangular body

C is for Cajon

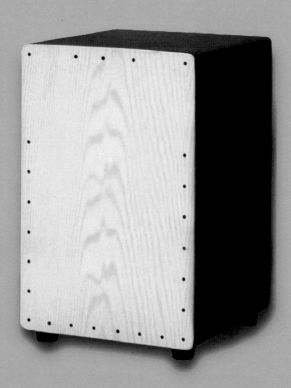

Is a box drum originated in Peru,
in the 16th century

D is for Didjeridoo

Australian wind instrument
It may be the world's oldest
musical instrument, over 40,000 years old

E is for Ektara

One-string instrument most often used in traditional music from India

F is for **Flute**

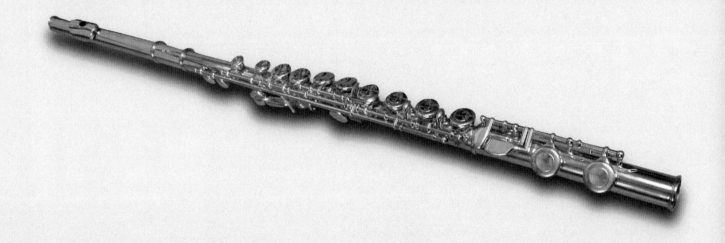

A number of flutes dating to about
43,000 to 35,000 years ago
have been found in the Swabian Jura
region of present-day Germany

G is for Guitar

A plucked stringed instrument with an almost 4000 years history

H is for Harp

One of the earliest harps was found in a wall painting of ancient Egyptian tombs dating from as early as 3000 B·C

I is for Istarski Mih

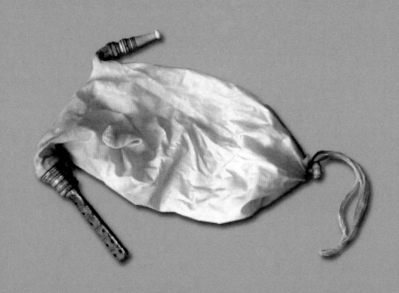

A bagpipe native to the regions of
Istria and Kvarner, Croatia

J is for Janggu

*The most widely used drum,
used in the traditional music of Korea*

K is for Koto

Traditional Japanese stringed instrument, derived from the Chinese zheng

L is for Lute

In the Renaissance era, the lute was the most popular instrument in the Western world

M is for Marimba

*A percussion instrument from Guatemala
The word marimba means
"the wood that sings"*

N is for Nay

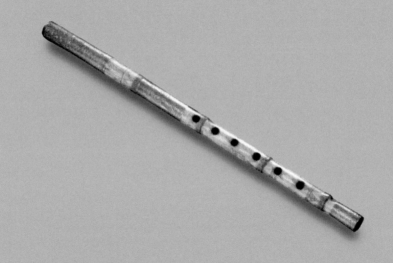

Nay is an old Persian word for reed
It is one of the oldest musical instruments
(4,500-5,000 years) still in use

O is for Oboe

The first woodwind instrument to be
included in the orchestras
of the 17th century, was created in France

P is for Piano

The first piano was invented in
Florence, Italy
in 1700 by Bartolomeo Cristofori

Q is for Quissange

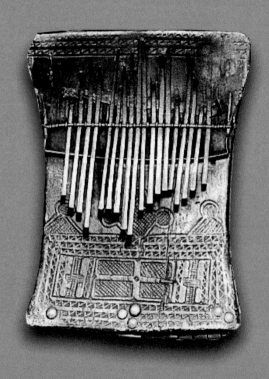

An idiophone musical instrument from Angola

R is for Recorder

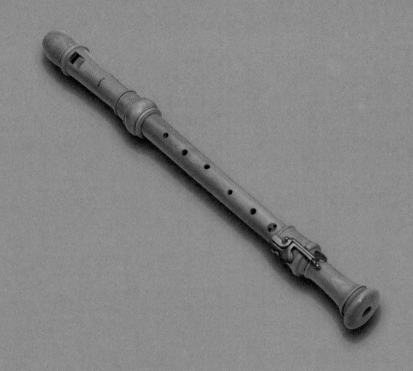

A woodwind instrument that dates from 1388 called "Recordour"

S is for Saxophone

Made of brass and invented by the Belgian instrument maker Adolphe Sax in 1840

T is for Tuba

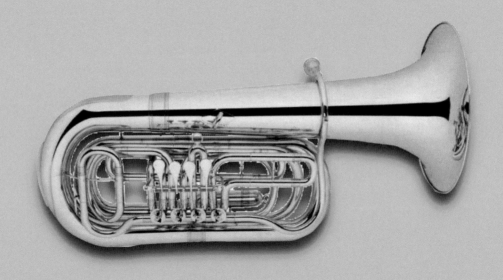

Is the largest and lowest-pitched
instrument in the brass family
It first appeared in the mid 19th-century

U is for Ukalele

A small guitar-like instrument that introduced to Hawaii by Portuguese immigrants in the 19th century

V is for Violin

A bowed stringed instrument that was first known in 16th-century Italy

W is for Waj

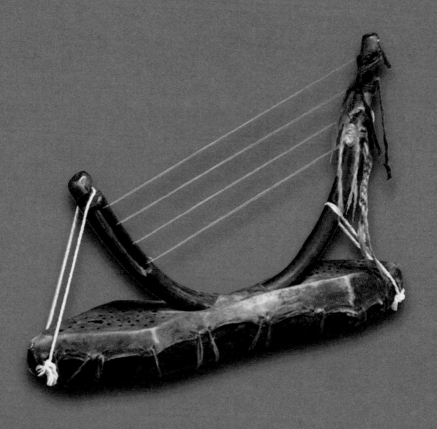

Spotted in Afghanistan. It was played during social gatherings, and to accompany epic storytelling or songs of heroic tales

X is for Xylophone

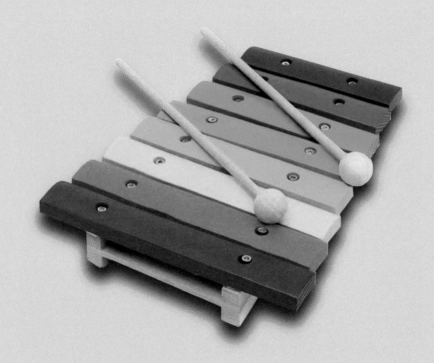

The earliest evidence of a true xylophone is from the 9th century in southeast Asia

Y is for   Yang Qin

A Chinese hammered dulcimer,
originally from Persia

Z is for Zither

The earliest known surviving instrument
of the zither family
is Chinese dating from 433 BC

Made in the USA
San Bernardino, CA
24 January 2020